DAY TRADING PROFIT PLAYBOOK:

Day Trading Strategies & Tactics to Make Money Trading Stocks - Understand Setup Patterns, Candlesticks, Money Management, & Market Trading Psychology!

KEN TURNER

Table of Contents

Introduction 1

Chapter 1: Getting Started - Mapping out your
          Day Trading Strategy 3

Chapter 2: How to Choose the Right Stocks to Trade 14

Chapter 3: Introduction to Candlesticks 22

Chapter 4: Charting for Beginners 33

Chapter 5: The Strategy Guide 50

Chapter 6: Stock Scanning & Building a Watchlist 59

Conclusion 63

Introduction

Congratulations on purchasing *Day Trading Profit Playbook*, and thank you for doing so. Day trading successfully is a long way from simply making a successful trade every now and then, and it requires plenty of hard work and dedication if you ever hope to do it successfully in either the short or the long-term. In return for all your effort, the potential for substantial return is greater than with any other type of trading.

While the road to success can be rocky, the following chapters will discuss everything you need to know about day trading in order to ensure you get started off on the right foot. First, you will learn about the basics of day trading, how to create a personalized trading plan that works for you, and common mistakes that new day traders make as well as how to ensure you don't follow suit. Next, you will learn how to start separating the stock heroes from the zeroes and keep it up indefinitely. You will then learn all about candlestick charts and how they will help you find success in the short-term.

From there, you will learn about a wide variety of technical indicators as well as strategies for making the most of each. You will then learn about a wide variety of strategies covering momentum trading, reversal trading, and more. Finally, you will learn how to make a shortlist of stocks to keep an eye on with tips for stock scanning and building a successful watchlist.

With so many choices out there, when it comes to consuming this type of content, it is appreciated that you've chosen this one. Plenty of care and effort went into ensuring it contains as many interesting and useful tidbits as possible. Please enjoy!

CHAPTER 1:

Getting Started - Mapping out your Day Trading Strategy

On a purely surface level, day trading is much the same as any other type of securities trading, just faster and for typically larger stakes. Day traders tend to hold positions they buy into for only a few minutes at a time, at most, with positions never being held longer than overnight, and even then, just in rare cases. As such, in order to become a successful day trader, you need to have experience trading in the stock market in a more traditional way, in addition to a high degree of discipline and dedication to your new way of trading.

The process of day trading can be broken down into 5 steps that will always be the same regardless of the specifics of the trade that is being made. First, you will need to locate an underlying stock that you are interested in trading based on research done ahead of time. Next, you will need to determine if it aligns with your personalized trading plan. Then, assuming you are still interested in making the trade, you will take a position based on the current trend of the market before buying or selling once a specific type of movement occurs. Finally, you will repeat this process roughly 100 times a day.

When it comes to day trading as a profession, day traders are classified in one of two ways: those who are lone traders and those who trade for large firms. The traders who work for larger institutions are typically going to have access to a wide variety of tools that other traders can only dream of. This high degree of access means that they can focus on trades that are going to generate an easy profit as they will have access to information the second it becomes public, allowing them to act on it while lone traders are still confirming the information they have received.

On the other hand, lone day traders are going to be much more well-equipped than the average small-time investor; otherwise, they are not going to be able to compete with other lone traders on an even playing field. They are often looking for the same types of trades as those traders who work for large firms, but their more limited resources mean that they are almost always going to need to take a higher degree of risk to achieve the same level of results.

While the previous description may make day trading sound like a relatively simple process, the truth of the matter is that it is an extremely complicated amalgamation of a wide variety of factors that not everyone has the time or mental fortitude to pursue on a regular basis. The following is a list of pros and cons that will hopefully make it easier to decide if it is really a path you want to follow or if there isn't another type of trading that will make it easier for you to reach your financial goals.

Pros

- Large profit margins: For those who do it right, day trading can be a very profitable career path with profits that are greater and more reliable than just about any other type of securities trading.

- Work for yourself: Many of the most successful day traders are self-employed, which means they don't have to answer to anyone. They can make their own hours and set their own profit goals.

- Always exciting: Dealing with the shortest market timeframes means that day traders typically see more action than any other type of securities trader. You will have the opportunity to pit your wits against the market as well as your competition each and every day. Those who are natural thrill seekers will also appreciate the adrenaline rush that comes from rapid-fire trading and pulling a big win from the grip of defeat.

- No degree required: As opposed to many other financial jobs, a perfectly successful day trader can be completely self-taught. As long as you are willing to put in the time and energy to learn the skills you need, you can be a success with no expensive courses or degree required. Everything you need to learn can be found online for free.

- Tax write off: As self-employed individuals, day traders can write off plenty of their expenses when it comes time to pay taxes. Hardware, software, and even home office space can all be written off by those who work from home.

Cons

- Commissions limit profits: Day traders have a much higher overall trade volume than other types of traders, which naturally means that their expenses in this arena are going to be much higher than other types of traders. While there are ways to minimize these costs, there is no denying that day trading is not for those with a smaller overall bankroll.

- Discipline is of the utmost importance: When it comes to day trading successfully, being able to stick with your trading plan, even amid emotional turmoil, is of the utmost importance. This attribute is prized in this scenario simply because it is so easy to misstep and wipe out a day's hard work in a matter of seconds.

Build a trading strategy that works for you

The fact of the matter is that there is simply no way you can expect to be successful in the long term when it comes to day trading if you don't have a plan that has been personalized based on your very own strengths and weaknesses. While skipping this section and finding a generalized trading plan online may be the fastest way to start trading as soon as possible, it is far from the most efficient.

Determine your current level of skill: In order to ensure that you create a plan with a realistic chance for success, the first thing that you are going to want to do is determine what your current competencies are when it comes to trading in general, and the underlying asset you are hoping to focus on specifically. The more experience you have, the more elaborate and ambitious your plan can be. But it is important to determine your level of experience, as overestimating your experience is only going to make it more difficult for you to start turning a profit in the first place.

Consider other obstacles: While you will likely have a few personal issues that may need to be worked through in order to achieve options trading success, it is important also to consider any other obstacles that might be standing in your way so that you can approach them properly. These obstacles can be anything from the limited amount of time that you are ultimately going to have to work with to simply not having the level of capital you would prefer in order to get started in the most effective way possible. It doesn't matter what the barrier is; it only matters how you are going to circumvent it. Having a clear idea of what may get in the way of your future success will allow you to prepare for it ahead of time and mitigate its long-term impact as much as possible. Taking the time to work through this step properly will help improve not only your overall success rate, but your bankable profits as well.

Decide how much risk is right for you: When it comes to determining how much risk is the right amount, the final solution is going to be different for each trader. This is because no singular amount of risk is perfect for everyone; risk is more individualized than that. To get started figuring out the ideal amount of risk for you, the first thing that you will want to do is to determine how much capital you are going to allot solely for trading, as well as what that amount means to you. If you have saved a few thousand dollars in a month or so to give something new a try, then your overall risk is going to be low. If you saved that same amount over nearly a year of dedicated saving, then that same amount might represent a much higher risk. Regardless, it is important never to put more into a single trade than you can ever afford to lose.

Set clear goals: When it comes to creating a starter trading strategy, you are going to want to consider not just your short-term goals, but also those that are more long-term as well. This means you are going to want to ensure that each trade you make clearly fits into your plan and automatically dismiss those that don't, even if they appear tempting at face value. When it comes to setting goals, it is essential that you ensure they are attainable and realistic, which means factoring in any real-life limitations that may apply. Goals that require hard work and dedication are motivating, and goals that are forever out of reach will eventually have a negative effect on your motivation.

Additionally, you are going to want to ensure that the goals you set are specific, which means setting goals with clear instances of success and failure for three months, six months, and a year down the line. Having a strict timeline will make it easier for you to follow through on your goals as you know exactly when you will have failed if you don't get to work. This means you will want to carefully consider all the logistics related to meeting your goals, as well as anything that may be standing between you and completing the goal successfully. Remember, the more specific you are when it comes to setting your goals, the more likely you are to actually achieve them. Remember, there is nothing more important than having a timeline set up from the get-go as, if your goals don't have timeframes, it will be much easier to put them off overall.

Keep track of your progress: When you first make your way into the world of day trading, it is important you track your progress to ensure that you don't start off on the wrong foot. This means you are going to want to track all of the details of each and every trade that you make for closer analysis at a later date. Depending on how useful you find this process early on, you may even want to continue it on into the foreseeable future. This means that you are going to want to track the time and date of each trade, the relevant financial specifics, why you choose the option in question, your emotional state, how long you held the option for, and the end result of the trade.

Just because you are tracking your trades doesn't mean you need to constantly be pouring over the results. Give yourself at least a month before checking in the first time to give true patterns the time they need to emerge. When you do check in, remember that anything over 50 percent is worth improving upon, while anything beneath that benchmark should be reworked completely.

Mistakes to Avoid

Forgetting that supply and demand still apply: While many day traders rely on extremely complicated metrics to determine what trades to make and when it is important to keep in mind that the market still runs on the basic principles of supply and demand that it always did. As such, if you cut through the complicated theories and look for moments where supply and demand are extremely unbalanced, then you will always be able to make a profit, no matter what. You will still need to learn as much as possible about the various strategies that you choose to move forward with. It is just essential to keep in mind that the basics still apply.

Not using daily limits: While always sticking to trades that have an acceptable amount of risk is the key to never losing more than you can afford to in a single go, it is also only half of the battle. Additionally, you are going to want to ensure that you have specific limits in mind when it comes to how much you can lose in a single day. While you might not feel that this is necessary, the fact of the matter is that it is very easy for your mental fortitude to begin to falter amid losses greater than 10 percent of your total day trading fund. This means that if you find yourself down this much, the best course of action is to hold off on trading any more for the rest of the day to allow yourself to get back on track. If you do find yourself down this much in a given day, it is equally important not to overestimate the importance of that fact. One bad day doesn't mean you need to rethink your entire plan; it only means that the market, whichever market you favor, is a fickle mistress.

Not starting early: Despite the fact that the New York Stock Exchange doesn't open until 9:30 am Eastern time, that doesn't mean that successful day traders start their days at that time. Instead, it is vital to use as much time prior to when the market opens as possible to ensure that you are prepared for any contingency that you can realistically expect the market to throw at you.

Remember, the markets that you choose to trade in do not exist in a vacuum. Global markets influence everything from the price of individual trades to the major players' views on the entire market, and if you go into the situation blind, then you will run the risk of finding yourself trading against the major players, an unenviable position under the best of circumstances and one that it will be impossible to pull a win from if you aren't even aware that you are doing it in the first place.

Not committing for the long haul: If conventional wisdom is to be believed, then you are going to need to practice trading in your market of choice for a full 10,000 hours before you can expect to be considered a master at what it is you are doing. As such, if you are trading regularly day in and day out, 5 days a week, 8 hours a day, then you can expect to really have a firm grasp on everything that is required of you in order to be successful in the long term in just 3 years and 6 months.

While this might seem like a serious commitment, it may be easier to swallow if you think of day trading as a marathon, rather than a race. Just because there are publicized stories of people making millions after just starting out in the day trading game, if you hope to maintain the motivation required to excel at the task at hand, it is important to not just know on the top level that they are the exception to the rule, but really believe that this is the truth as well.

CHAPTER 2:

How to Choose the Right Stocks to Trade

While it should come as no surprise that you are going to need to gather as much data as possible in order to make the best trades, regardless of what market you are working in; it is important to keep in mind that if you don't use it in the right way, then it is all for naught. There are two ways to get the most out of any of the data that you gather; the first is via technical analysis and the second is via fundamental analysis. As a general rule, you will likely find it helpful to start off with fundamental analysis before moving on to technical analysis as the need arises.

To understand the difference between the two, you may find it helpful to think about technical analysis as analyzing charts while fundamental analysis looks at specific factors based on the underlying asset for the market that you are working in. The core tenant of fundamental analysis is that there are related details out there that can tell the whole story when it comes to the market

Conclusion

Thanks for making it through to the end of *Day Trading Profit Playbook*, I hope it was informative and able to provide you with all of the tools you need to achieve your goals, whatever it is that they may be. Just because you've finished this book doesn't mean there is nothing left to learn about the topic, and expanding your horizons is the only way to find the mastery you seek.

Now that you have made it to the end of this book, you hopefully have an understanding of how to get started taking your first steps into the world of day trading, as well as a strategy or two, or three, that you are anxious to try for the first time. Before you go ahead and start giving it your all; however, it is important that you have realistic expectations as to the level of success you should expect in the near future.

While it is perfectly true that some people experience serious success right out of the gate, it is an unfortunate fact of life that they are the exception rather than the rule. What this means is that you should expect to experience something of a learning curve, especially when you are first figuring out what works for you. This is perfectly normal; however, if you persevere, you will come out the other side better because of it. Instead of getting your hopes up to an unrealistic degree, you should think of your time spent with the stock market as a marathon rather than a sprint, which means that slow and steady will win the race every single time.

Finally, if you found this book useful in any way, a review is always appreciated!

in question while technical analysis believes that the only details that are required are those that relate to the price at the moment.

As such, fundamental analysis is typically considered easier to master, as it all relates to concepts less expressly related to understanding market movement exclusively. Meanwhile, technical analysis is typically faster because key fundamental analysis data often is only made publicly available on a strict, and limited, schedule, sometimes only a few times a year, meaning the availability for updating specific data is rather limited.

Fundamental analysis basics

The best time to use fundamental analysis is when you are looking to gain a broad idea of the state of the market as it stands and how that relates to the state of things in the near future when it comes time to actually trading successfully. Regardless of what market you are considering, the end goals are the same: find the most effective trade for the time period that you are targeting.

Establish a baseline: In order to begin analyzing the fundamentals, the first thing that you will need to do is to create a baseline regarding the company's overall performance. In order to generate the most useful results possible, the first thing that you are going to need to do is gather data both regarding the company in question as well as the related industry as a whole. When gathering macro data, it is important to keep in mind that no market is going to operate in a vacuum, which means the reasons behind the specific market movement can be much more far-reaching than they first appear. Fundamental analysis works because of the stock market's propensity for patterns, which means if you trace a specific market movement back to the source, you will have a better idea of what to keep an eye on in the future.

Consider worldwide issues: Once you have a general grasp on the current phase you are dealing with, the next thing you will want to consider is anything that is going on in the wider world that will alter the type of businesses you tend to favor in your stocks. Not being prepared for major paradigm shifts, especially while day trading, means that you can easily miss out on massive profits and should be avoided at all costs. To ensure you are not blindsided by news you could have seen coming, it is important to look beyond the obvious issues that are consuming the 24-hour news cycle and dig deeper into the comings and goings of the parts of the market that are going to be most affected by your favored stocks.

Look for historical precedents: Once you have a firm grasp on the present and a hypothetical grasp on the future, you are going to need to look to the past to see how it measures up. Looking back to how the industry you are considering has done historically will give you a better idea of the true strength of the current phase. When things are starting to look up, you can expect that credit will become easier to come by and erratic market movement is at a relatively low, which means it should be quite easy to turn a profit in nearly all sectors.

Consider competitive advantage: It is also important to consider the various competitive advantages that the company you have your eye on might have over its competition. Companies that are going to be successful in the long-term are always going to have an advantage over their competition in one of two ways. They can either have better operational effectiveness or improved strategic positioning. Operational effectiveness is the name given to doing the same things as the competition, but in a more efficient and effective way. Strategic positioning occurs when a company gains an edge by doing things that nobody else is doing.

Look to the leadership: The type of management that is currently leading a company is going to go a long way towards determining if it is going to be successful in the long run. After all, even the most well thought out business plan will fail if it isn't able to rely on the right infrastructure to support it in the long run. When it comes to analyzing management, the first place you are going to want to look is the corporate information section of the company's website. This won't provide you with much more than the names of the folks at the top, but if they have been around the block, then names should be enough to pull up everything you need to know about their past work experiences. While this might not ultimately amount to much, if there is something unfortunate in their past, this should bring it to light.

Technical analysis basics

Technical analysis is for you if you enjoy the idea of determining likely future performance based on previous price movements without having to dig through all of the paperwork that is associated with fundamental analysis. While the past will never be able to completely predict the future with perfect clarity, when it is combined with an understanding of market mentality, it can be an effective way to generate accurate predictions as long as you understand its shortcomings.

In order to properly understand technical analysis, the most important thing you need to keep in mind is that the action the price has taken to get to the current point is likely going to repeat itself in the future, which makes it a reliable way to predict future movement based on what is happening at the moment.

This fact makes it easy to use the tools of technical analysis, including trends, charts, and indicators to generate a reasonable successful trade percentage. While some of the ways that it works are more complicated than others, in its most basic form, technical analysis is all about the study of supply and demand, and it uses its findings to determine the type of trend, if any, that is affecting the market at the moment. This can prove crucial to your day trading success in the long-term as the tools at your disposal will become even more useful as you have your own historical data to sample as well.

Price charts: The key to unlocking everything that technical analysis can do lies in the price chart, which is a standard chart with an x- and a y-axis. The price is measured via the vertical axis and the time is measured on the horizontal axis. There are numerous different types of price charts out there, each with its own set of proponents; some of these charts include the line chart, the tick chart, the candlestick chart, the Heikin-Ashi chart, the bar chart, the Kagi chart, and the Renko chart. However, the ones you are going to be dealing with the most are likely going to be the point and click chart, the line chart, the candlestick chart, and the bar chart.

- Line chart: Of all the types of charts that are out there, the line chart is the simplest to use because it only presents a small slice of the potential information you will get from most other types of charts. Specifically, they show the closing price of the underlying asset you are following for a fixed period of time. The titular lines are formed when the closing price points are connected with a line.

- Bar chart: When compared to a line chart, a bar chart adds in the additional details related to a stock's movement throughout each day. The top and the bottom of the bar are going to represent the high and low for the day respectively, and the closing price is denoted by a dash found on the right side of the bar. Meanwhile, the dash on the left side of the bar is going to show the starting price. Finally, if the overall value of the stock increases for the day, then the bar will be black. And if it decreases, it will be either red or clear depending on your trading software.

- Candlestick chart: A candlestick is similar to a bar chart in many ways, though it also provides additional relevant information that is more detailed overall. It includes the range for the day, expressed as a line, as with a bar graph, but when you view a candlestick chart, you will also notice a wide bar near the vertical line, which indicates the degree of the difference the price experienced over a given period of time. If the price increases for the day, then the candlestick will not be shaded in, and if the price decreased throughout the day, then it will typically be shaded in red as well.

- Point and figure chart: While the point and figure chart are used less frequently than some of the charts that have been previously discussed, the point and figure chart has been in constant use for more than 100 years and can still provide insight when used correctly. Specifically, this chart is used to determine how much a price is likely to move without taking timing or volume into account. This makes it a pure indicator of price, without any of the market noise that might otherwise be attached. A point and figure chart can be easily picked out from the crowd as it is made up of Xs and Os rather than lines and points. The Xs will indicate the points where positive trends occurred while the Os will indicate periods of downward movement.

CHAPTER 3:

Introduction to Candlesticks

The modern candlestick chart first gained prominence in Japan more than 300 years ago. It was created by a futures market trader named Homma, who made the shocking discovery that while supply and demand played a part in price, the emotions of those who were trading were nearly as influential in the overall outcome. While Homma traded in rice futures, the truth that he came to is universal in all markets. Put simply, he realized that when emotions come into play, the real value of an asset and that same asset's perceived value can vary to an extreme degree and that principle remains true today.

This guiding principle is what has made candlestick charting so very popular with traders of all types, all around the world. Additionally, it only provides relative feedback when it comes to outlooks in the short term, which typically last no more than 10 total trading sessions. This doesn't mean that candlestick charting is simple; however, the parts of it can certainly seem difficult to understand at first. Thus, it is important to persevere, and things will become more clear in time.

In order to create an accurate candlestick, you need four different pieces of information. The first one is the amount the stock in question opened at, the second is the overall high for the day, the third is the overall low for the day, and the fourth is the price it closed at. From there, the data is plotted in such a way that it looks like a box with a line through it. The two endpoints of the line represent the high and low respectively when the top and bottom edges of the box represent the opening and closing prices respectively. Stocks that ended on an appreciation profit are one color, and those that suffered a loss are a second color.

Range: The range is a visual representation of the market's current level of volatility. The bigger the box is in relation to the line, also known as the wick, the more active the market currently is and the higher the overall degree of volatility. The greater the amount of volatility the market is currently experiencing, the higher the amount of risk. No clear bar means the market is currently uncertain, and you should wait for clear signals one way or another.

Body: Body refers to the physical orientation of the box in question. This means that if the close is above the open, then the market improved, and if the price closes underneath the open, then the market decreased in value. What's more; when looking at the box, you are going to want to take note of how large the box is in relation to the wick. The larger the box is in relation to the wick, the stronger the market is overall.

Top wick/bottom wick: After you have a clear idea of the body as well as the range of a candle, you are then able to accurately determine what the upper wick is telling you. The upper wick shows the uppermost point that the price reached in a given time frame that was unable to be matched by overall market movement. What this wick signifies is that after the price rose to the top point, the number of sellers was higher than the number of buyers, so the price dropped again instead of rising. Likewise, the lower wick indicates how strong the pressure to buy was on the stock in question.

Dual price bars: Once you decide to add a second price bar to the analysis that you are doing, you will then be able to use the dual price bars as a cornerstone that provides you with a reasonable idea of the level of movement the price is experiencing in a more practical sense than if you were looking at a single bar. The second bar will also allow you to more easily determine if what you found in the first bar is a fluke or something that is actually actionable enough to make a move on before it's too late. Eventually, you will likely find this exceptionally useful if you need to determine if a bar is actually wide or is, in fact, average or other forms of comparison as well. This will allow you to understand the price action in a way that is more specific, and thus more effective than it would often otherwise be.

Candlestick patterns

Long wick: One of the most common types of candlestick patterns is what is known as the long black line or simply the long black wick. When charting a candlestick pattern, if you see the long black wick, then you should know it indicates that the market is in a period of bearishness. This means that during the trading period that is being charted, the currency or currency pairs that you are charting moved both up and down in a wide range throughout the period being charted. Additionally, it can indicate that the price started near the high point for the day and ended at a point much lower, closer to the end of the day.

Alternatively, a long white wick indicates a period where the market was bullish, which means that the exact opposite, when compared with the long black wick, is true. This ultimately means that while the price of the currency or currencies in question moved through several whipsaw periods, the end result worked out to be that the start of the period saw lower prices while the end of the trading period was privy to higher prices overall.

Tweezer bottom candlestick pattern: The biggest indicator that a market is turning from trending to ranging is what is known as a tweezer bottom candlestick pattern. If this occurs at the same time as a Fibonacci retracement, notable pivot level, support, and resistance or round number, then you will know that the signal is even stronger still. You may be able to make a profit from taking a trade at this level, though you are typically going to want to wait for the confirmation of a ranging price through the telltale turn of the opposite band.

You can spot a tweezer bottom candlestick pattern because it is made up of two separate individual forex candles. The first candle, known as the setup candle, is either going to be notably bullish or bearish and will ideally occur at the tail end of a substantial price push down. This candle represents the last vestiges of the downward price surge and also a failure back from the low price.

The second candle is known as the confirmation candle and is always going to be bullish. The confirmation candle will have a peak price or lower wick that will match quite closely, or even exactly, with that of the setup candle. The stronger the signal, the greater the length of the confirmation candle wick. This represents the amount of low point rejection that is taking place.

The tweezer bottom candlestick pattern will most frequently occur at the end of a period of decreasing price regardless if that move represents a portion of a longer trend or just a short retracement. If it occurs at the tail end of a long-running decrease in price, then it indicates the supply of sellers is nearly exhausted. This, in turn, means that the market of buyers is eager for opportunities. When this occurs, the buyers will be much more inclined to jump into the market as the levels of the currency pair in question are sure to be quite cheap. If a bear and bull struggle is taking place, the bulls are typically going to come out on top. Once this happens, the price will generally settle near the high point of the confirmation candle and at a point above its opening.

Outside reversal: This is a price chart pattern that can be visible when the low and high for the day both exceed the high of the trading session of the previous day. This pattern is referred to as a bearish engulfing pattern if the second bar is a down candlestick, and a bullish engulfing pattern if the second bar is instead an up candlestick. This pattern typically proves useful if you need to identify the future price movement as well as determine if it is going to be positive or negative. It typically occurs at the point where the first price bar drops outside the range of the previous price bar when its high is above the previous high, and the low is as well. As a general rule, if the outside reversal occurs at the level of resistance, then the signal is bearish, and if it occurs at the support level, then it is bullish.

Hook reversal: The hook reversal pattern is most frequently found in charts with shorter timeframes. They can appear during any type of trend and are especially useful when it comes to learning about a new trend that will mark a reversal of the current status quo. This type of pattern is known to appear with a higher low as well as a lower high when compared to the candles of the previous day. You can tell this pattern from the rest because the size difference between the body of the first and second bar is quite small when compared to other, similar patterns.

If this type of pattern forms around a positive trend, then the open will naturally be nearer the previous high while the low will form near the previous low. This pattern is frequently associated with other more frequently seen positions as the body of the second candle will often form with the first candle's body. The strength you can attribute to this signal will often be tied directly to the overall strength of the trend with a stronger trend naturally having a stronger signal to give off.

Abandoned baby: This candlestick pattern can prove especially useful when it comes to determining points where a reversal might start within the current trend. This type of pattern is created from a trio of candlesticks with several distinctive characteristics. The first bar is going to be a red candlestick that is large and visible within a previously defined downtrend. The second bar will have an open equal to its close that gaps beneath the close of the first bar.

The final bar is going to be a white candlestick that is large and opens higher than the second bar. This bar also represents changing trader sentiment. This is a fairly unique pattern, but it can be used reliably if you are looking to predict a change to an existing downtrend. The accuracy of the signal will then be further enhanced when combined with additional technical indicators, such as the MACD and RSI.

The bearish abandoned baby is useful if you are curious if an existing positive trend is likely going to reverse sooner than later. It is also a type of trio pattern, and the first portion is the white candlestick that is found within the current positive trend. The second bar will be the same as that in the middle of the bullish abandoned baby, and the final bar will be a large red candle that will open somewhere below the second bar.

Mind the gap: When you come across a candlestick with a gap in it, then you can safely assume that the price of that particular asset will have moved quickly from one point to another that is either much higher or lower in order to create it. As this much movement, all at once, is relatively uncommon, coming across one should be enough to give you pause and cause you to look at the asset that caused the gap more closely.

Over time, you will find that identifying the gap early on will allow you to make a wide variety of different predictions based on what the market was up to at the time. These include:

If the gap is created during a period of low trading volume, then it is likely that the gap price will be corrected very quickly. This type of gap is generally formed after a large trade goes through after most of the institutional traders have called it a day. This means that the change doesn't actually reflect the strengths of the underlying asset so that you can easily set up binary contracts that take advantage of the fact that things will soon be moving back towards normal.

If the gap occurs during a stretch where overall trade volume is up but the movement on the underlying asset in question has been neutral, then this can be thought of as a strong indicator that a new breakout is occurring, which means that the potential for profits is increased. If you move quickly, you can take advantage of this fact by buying into contracts that line up with the direction the breakout indicates.

Finally, if the gap appears during a space of average trading volume when the asset in question is already moving in a given direction, then the gap can be thought of as a sign that the trend that it is being monitored is accelerating. This, in turn, means that the trend is likely to continue, at least in the short-term. You will only want to be comfortable assuming the trend is going to last into a longer timeframe if ancillary indicators are very strong.

Additional types of gaps to look out for include:

Breakaway gap: This type of gap is used to describe a situation where the price of a given stock either gaps over a resistance or support level. This type of price gap often leads to breakouts and additional bullish movement.

- Exhaustion gap: This scenario typically forms after a substantial trend has already occurred. It is generated when the price makes one final jump in the direction of the prevalent trend and then reverses dramatically.

- Common gap: As the name indicates, a common gap is the most frequently seen gap, which occurs without typically indicating much of anything when it comes to the overall movement. Common gaps occur most frequently when the price of a given stock is ranging. They are typically not very large and, as such, tend to fill in quite quickly.

- Continuation gap: This situation most frequently takes place in a trend that is already taking place. If it occurs during an uptrend, then it indicates the trend is likely to continue as it marks the point that additional buyers jumped into the market, pushing the price to greater heights in the process. The same can be said for a downward trend and new sellers entering the market.

- Full gap: This type of gap frequently occurs when the price at the open of the current day is dramatically different than that of the previous day. It occurs as a positive if a starting price of a given stock is greater than the high point that price reached sometime the day before. Likewise, a negative full gap appears if the starting price is below the lowest point from the previous trading day.

- Partial gap: This type of gap occurs when there has been a moderate amount of change between the price between yesterday at close and today's open. A partial gap occurs when the price at open is greater than yesterday's price at close, but is not greater than the previous day's high. A partial gap down occurs when the price at open is lower than yesterday's close, but not greater than yesterday's overall low.

CHAPTER 4:

Charting for Beginners

It can be difficult for many traders, especially those who are just getting used to technical analysis, to see the somewhat hidden signs that are pointing towards buy or sell that are often sitting right in front of them, which can lead to them sitting on the sidelines while profitable trades pass them by. What these types of traders are failing to understand is that there is no one right way to trade, which means you are going to need to consider several different types of technical indicators if you hope to use technical analysis to bring in the profits you have always dreamed of. While there are many types of technical indicators that you could consider, the following are the ones you should get familiar with first, before expanding your horizons as desired from there.

Before you can start utilizing them effectively, however, it might help to have a better idea of what a technical indicator is exactly. Specifically, a technical indicator, sometimes referred to as a tool, is one of a variety of different metrics whose value is inherently tied to the current price of a given currency or currency pair. The goal of all technical indicators, though some do their job better than others, is to determine the direction the price of a given currency or currency pair is going to move as well as the degree of that movement, if possible. This is done by analyzing past patterns through a wide variety of ways discussed in the following chapters.

Also called technicals, technical indicators are easy to spot once you know what to look for because they do not inherently analyze any of the fundamentals related to the country or countries in question. Instead, they are used to analyze movements in price, primarily in the short term. When it comes to long term investing, technical indicators tend to be less useful as they don't often have access to a wide enough breadth of data to provide insight into the future in that way. As such, long term investors are typically known to use technical indicators as a way of determining the right entry points to take advantage of and the right exit points to have in place to prevent financial disaster.

Technical indicators tend to come in two main types: lagging and leading. Lagging indicators are those that are based on preceding data and help to determine when a trend is forming or if a stock is currently trading in range instead. The stronger the trend the lagging indicator pinpoints, the greater the chance that it is going to continue moving forward. However, lagging indicators are of no use when it comes to determining future rally points or potential pullbacks.

Alternately, leading indicators are useful when it comes to predicting the point where the price of a given stock may rally or crash. These are typically momentum indicators, which gauge the momentum of the movement the price of an underlying stock is likely to take. A momentum indicator can be thought of as the common sense that says a ball thrown into the air will not continue in the same direction forever. Once it begins to slow down, you can accurately predict that it will soon begin to move in the opposite direction.

Leading indicators are useful when it comes to determining if the price of an underlying stock has reached an unsustainable point and when likely slowdown of a given price will occur. As stocks that are overbought or oversold are in for a pullback, having this information before the move occurs can be extremely useful when used with numerous trading strategies.

Both types of indicators are equally important as you will need to determine what types of trends are going to be forming and as well be on the lookout for eventual slowdowns and pullbacks at any time in order to use many strategies successfully. Typically, you are going to want to use at least three indicators at all times.

Stick with the trends

While advanced traders tend to find more success trading against the trends of the market, when you are first getting started with technical analysis, it is far easier to go with the flow and trade in the direction the market is trending. This will still require some practice, however, especially if you don't already have a means of determining which trends are going to appear where. While some people will swear that a trend following tool is really all you need to get started trading successfully, in reality, they are only really helpful when it comes to helping you to determine if the right choice in the current market is to enter into a long position or if a short position is a better choice. One of the easiest, and as a result most reliable, trend measuring tools to use is what is generally referred to as the moving average crossover.

Traditional moving average: The crossover point is the place on the chart where a given underlying asset, along with the indicator you are using to track it, intersect with each other. As such, the moving average crossover is a simple way for traders to keep tabs on when the current trend might start to change. A moving average is a type of technical indicator that makes it easier for a trader to predict the price movement of a specific underlying asset by smoothing out the rough edges. It is what is known as a lagging indicator, which means that it can only ever function to show you where the price has been, as opposed to where it is going.

Simple moving average: The simple moving average is actually a little more complicated than the traditional moving average because it also calculates the price of the specific underlying asset over several different timeframes before dividing the total by the number of time periods that are being used in the process. When using this process, it is common for successful traders to keep an eye out for averages in the short-term to cross the point that is greater than the existing average over an extended period of time, which is a good sign that an uptrend is incoming.

Confirmation indicators

After you have a clear idea as to how to determine if the underlying assets you are considering are currently part of a positive or negative trend, then you will need to consider a technical indicator that will make it easier for you to confirm that the trend you are looking at is going to prove to be as useful as you may have initially hoped. This type of indicator is especially useful as the trends that are uncovered via the simple moving average are often prone to extreme periods of sporadic movement that can be difficult to compensate for, even if you know it is coming. As such, a secondary tool for trend confirmation can be useful to ensure that you don't waste time on trends that are not ultimately going to pan out.

The purpose of this tool is not to then generate buy or sell signals related to a given underlying asset, but instead to agree or disagree with the trend-following tool you decide to use. As such, when both tools result in a confirmed bullish market, then you can feel more confident when you choose a long trade related to the underlying assets you are curious in learning more about. The same goes for a doubly confirmed bearish market and short selling the pair that you have chosen. The most commonly used confirmation tool is one that is referred to as the moving average convergence divergence or MACD for short. This tool measures the amount of difference there is between two averages that have been smoothed to minimize ancillary noise.

The difference between the two results is then further smoothed by the process before then being matched against the moving average that it relates to as well. If the resulting smoothed average is still greater than the existing moving average, then you can be sure that the positive trend you were chasing actually exists. Meanwhile, if the smoothed average ends up below the existing moving average, then any negative trends will be confirmed instead.

MACD: The moving average convergence divergence indicator is a type of oscillating indicator that primarily moves between zero and the centerline. If the MACD value is high, then you can assume the related underlying asset is nearly overbought, and if the value is low, then the stock is nearly oversold.

The MACD chart is typically based on a combination of several EMAs. These averages can be based on any timeframe, though the most common is the 12-26-9 chart. This chart is typically broken into multiple parts, the first of which is the 26-day and 12-day chart. Mixing up the EMAs will allow you to more accurately gauge the level of momentum that the trend you are tracking is experiencing.

If the 12-day EMA ends up above the 26-day EMA, then you can assume the underlying stock in an uptrend, and the reverse indicates a downtrend. If the 12-day EMA increases more quickly than the 26-day EMA, then the uptrend is going to be even more well-pronounced. However, if the 12-day EMA moves closer to the 26-day EMA, then you can safely assume that it is starting to slow, and the momentum is waning, which means it is going to take the trend with it.

The MACD uses the EMA by considering the difference between them once they are plotted out. If the 26-day and the 12-day are the same, then the MACD equal out to 0. If the 12-day ends up at a higher point than the 26-day, then you can assume the MACD is positive; if not, it will be negative.

From there, you will then want to take into account the 9-day EMA as well. The 9-day EMA is different in that it determines the trend of the AMCD line as opposed to that of the stock price. As such, if the 9-day EMA smooths out the movement of the MACD line, the results are going to be far more manageable.

If the result then generates a trend that indicates a negative amount of divergence, then you can be quite certain that the positive trend that is currently taking place is ultimately going to hit a level of resistance that it simply won't be able to overcome. This, in turn, means that it will have to reverse sooner rather than later.

The 5-minute MACD entry strategy works in the 5-minute chart and utilizes a pair of MACDs along with a pair of moving averages. The moving averages are a 50 bar and a 100 bar. The pair of MACDs are both the common 12-day and 26-day with the 9-day signal bar. The first is a histogram and the second is an oscillator. When combined, the two can accurately create signals with movements that last from 20 minutes to many hours.

The pair of moving averages are then used to determine the current trend, as well as the type of trade that you will want to make and also as part of the signal for when you will want to enter the trade. In this case, the trend is determined by the position of the moving averages. If the 50 bar moving average is higher than the 100 bar moving average, then you know the trend is bullish, and you will want to place a call. If the short-term moving average is lower than the long-term moving average, then the trend is bearish, and you will want to place a put.

The signal to move forward is created when the MACD is either oversold or overbought and is indicated by a crossover at the same time the prices have moved past the moving averages. If the trend is moving downward, then you will want to wait for the prices to correct to a point above the moving averages before entering. This will coincide with a signal created by the oscillator MACD, which will show on the overbought side of things and create a bearish crossover. This signal, in turn, will be predicted by the histogram MACD. The opposite is true for bullish signals.

If used on the 5-minute chart, then you will want to target either a 20 or 30-minute expiration point, depending on how strong overall you believe the current trend is going to be. If you are using the 30-minute chart, then you would set the expiration at between 2 and 3 hours. If you are using the daily charts, then you will want to put the expiration point at between 4 days and 1 week.

RSI: The relative strength index (RSI) is typically used to calculate results in increments of three days and measures the total sum of positive days and negative days before calculating a value with a range between 0 and 100. If the movement of the asset in question during this period is generally positive, then the indicator will end up closer to 100, and if the movement is negative, the result will be closer to 0. As such, if the result is close to 50, then the results are considered to be neutral.

Stochastic: The stochastic oscillator is a type of momentum indicator that compares the closing price of an underlying asset to the range of prices it achieved over a specific period of time. The sensitivity of this oscillator to specific movements of the market can be reduced by adjusting the time period or through the process of taking a moving average of its results.

The stochastic oscillator also plays an important role when it comes to determining if a specific underlying asset is oversold or overbought due to the fact that it remains range bound. Its range is between 0 and 100 and will always remain constant regardless of how quickly or slowly the underlying asset moves. The traditional setting of this oscillator is 20 as the oversold threshold with the overbought threshold appearing at 80.

A/D Line: The Advance-Decline (A/D) Line is an indicator for breadth that takes into account net advances, which is the number of underlying assets in a given market that are seeing gains when compared to those who are seeing losses. The line can then be used to compare the expected performance of the market as a whole compared to how it is actually doing. When bearish or bullish divergences are found in the A/D line, it is a signal that a reversal could be on the horizon.

The accumulation and distribution line has both benefits and drawbacks you should be aware of. First and foremost, it makes it easier to monitor the overall money flow as it can easily be used to gauge the current flow of money. If the accumulation and distribution line is increasing, then this will signal that buying pressure is winning out. On the contrary, if the accumulation and distribution line has a downward trajectory, then this shows that selling pressure is winning out. It can also be useful when it comes to determining the strength and longevity of a move that is already occurring.

On the other hand, the accumulation and distribution line has a few drawbacks, including the fact that it doesn't do well with trading gaps. The accumulation and distribution line doesn't consider trading gaps at all, which means that if the price of the stock in question gaps while moving upward and then still closes at the midpoint, the accumulation and distribution line won't show it as it is only concerned with closing prices. Oftentimes, it can also be difficult to detect minor changes in the volume flow when using the accumulation and distribution line. When a trend begins to slow, but not stop, then you won't know until the accumulation and distribution line begins to actually move in the other direction.

In order to determine either bullish or bearish signals, you need to first determine the trend in the stock you are keeping tabs on. After this has been found, you can then look for the divergence in the trend as described above. When looking for these types of divergences, you are going to want to look at weekly charts as the signals can often take an extended period of time to develop. Signs that indicate a bearish pattern is on the rise include signals that do not have a sharp divergence or are otherwise flat in general. These signs can also indicate that there may be no real change in the near future.

Average directional index: The average directional index can be thought of as a guidepost that confirms the signals that other technical indicators bring to light. After a trend has been successfully identified, the average directional index can then more easily determine its strength compared to the other trends that are currently taking place. The average directional index is a combination of directional indicators that are both negative and positive and thus can more easily track trends regardless of their direction. They are then unified in a way that determines the overall strength of the trend.

As an oscillating indicator, the average directional index ranges between 100 and 0. The low end indicates that the trend is essentially flat and without volatility, while the high end indicates that the stock is virtually moving straight up and down very quickly. This indicator is only useful when it comes to measuring the overall strength of the trend, not which direction it is moving in or is likely to move in any time soon.

As a general rule, it is rare to see an average directional index value above 60. This is due to the fact that trends with that much strength are only likely to appear during periods of a deep recession or extremely long bullish market runs. What this means is that a value of anything greater than 40 can be considered a vibrant trend, and anything lower than 20 indicates an underlying stock within the trading range.

When watching for average directional index signals, if a trend moves from above 40 to below it, then you can assume the current trend is slowing, which means it may be time to mix up your current trading strategy or close out any existing positions. However, if you see a trend start at less than 20 and then increase to a point near 40, then you will know that a neutral market is starting to pick up steam and a major trend is likely going to be formed.

It is also important to always keep in mind the point where both the negative and positive directional indices cross. If the negative directional index is crossed by the positive in an upward direction, then you can assume the market is feeling bullish.

Pivots: The daily pivots indicator is simple and yet very effective; therefore, the identified probable outcomes in any given situation are materialized for most cases. Professional foreign exchange traders and makers of the market use the pivot point indicator to predict the potential resistance and support levels. Summarily, pivot points and their support/resistance levels indicate areas at which the price movement direction might change.

The main reason for most traders finding pivot points enticing is that they are objective. Unlike most of the other indicators, pivot points do not involve discretion. There are many similarities between pivot points and Fibonacci levels. However, the two differ in that Fibonacci involves some subjectivity when one is picking the swing highs and the swing lows. When the price is trading on the lower side of the pivot point, then it indicates that the day is negative or bearish. When the price is trading on the upper side of the pivot point, then it indicates that the day is positive or bullish.

The pivot point indicator typically involves four extra levels, namely R1, S1, R2, and S2. They basically mean resistance 1, Support 1, Resistance 2, and support 2. The resistance and support may cause reversals, and a trader may also use them as a confirmation of the trend. For instance, if a trader sees that the price is falling gradually and moving below S1, he/she confirms a downtrend, and this indicates a possible continuation to support 2.

Pivot points are intraday indicators for trading in the stock trading market. Pivot points normally remain at the same price throughout the day and are very static compared to Oscillators and moving averages. This means that a trader will be able to use the levels when planning out a trade in advance. For instance, the traders know that if the price goes below the pivot point, chances are, they will sell early in the session. If the price goes above the pivot point, then the trader is likely to buy. The first and second resistance and support can be used as stop-loss levels and target prices.

Traders get pivot points based on simple calculations. The simplicity is perfect for some traders, but some other traders might see it pretty useless. Again, there is no way of guaranteeing the price will reverse, stop at, or even attain the levels that are created on the charts. At other times, the price of the asset will move up and down through a level. It is best if a trader uses the indicator as part of a larger trading plan.

A trader can calculate pivot points either on a daily, weekly, monthly, or yearly basis. Under normal circumstances, short-term traders such as scalpers and day traders use the daily pivot points, while the medium-term traders, for instance, the swing traders focus on the monthly and weekly pivot points. Long-term traders can use the yearly points and maybe combine them with the monthly points.

Traders need to know that all higher scale pivot points are beneficial for all traders regardless of their short-term or long-term trade decision. As such, a scalper and day trader will benefit more if he/she knows where the daily, weekly, monthly, and even yearly points are situated on the charts. This is because the market will stop and reverse at these points.

Traders and makers of the market have used the pivot points for many years to determine the crucial resistance or support levels. The main reason why the pivot points are so popular in the Stock trading market is that currencies tend to fluctuate. Range-bound traders enter a buy order close to the identified level of support and will enter a sell order when the price nears the resistance. These points also help the breakout and trend traders to identify the key levels that must be broken. Furthermore, the technical levels can become handy as the market opens.

Having an awareness of the places that these turning points are located enables an individual investor to be more attuned to the market and the price movements, thus making more educated decisions about transactions. With the identified ease of calculation, the pivot points can be incorporated into a lot of trading strategies. There are flexibility and simplicity with the pivot points, and as such, a trader can add them to their trading toolbox.

CHAPTER 5:

The Strategy Guide

Momentum trading

A majority of the traders in the stock trading market tend to feel confused, especially in the initial stages of their endeavors. They feel and know that they can make money, but have a challenge achieving success with consistency. As such, some traders start blaming the market saying that it is too random and there are cheating brokers in the field who make traders suffer.

However, these are just excuses in most cases. One thing for sure is that the market has patterns and it is not random. Even though a broker can be less than perfect when trading, a trader can still generate profits if he/she stops thinking about blaming the market and apply a good approach to the trading activities. Momentum trading style is one of the methods used to choose currency pairs that will produce positive results.

Momentum in stock trading simply states that one should buy an underlying asset if the price is going up and sell it when it is going down. In other words, a trader using a momentum strategy is seeking to capitalize on the continuation of an existing trend in the market. Some academic researchers have found that applying the principle of momentum in trades and markets is actually very profitable over time and a trader gets a winning trading edge.

There is another type of momentum strategy referred to as 'best of' trading strategy. This strategy buys the assets that are strongly going up and selling those that are going down more strongly than others. This strategy also works very well for traders and tends to give a greater risk/reward ratio compared to simple momentum strategies. Traders base their decisions to buy or sell on the strength of the recent price trends.

The momentum in stock trading trade is very similar to that of physics, whereby the mass is multiplied by velocity to determine the possibility that the object will continue on the current path. However, in the financial markets, the determinants of momentum include trade volume and the rate at which prices are changing. A momentum trader bets that the price of a particular asset that is moving in a given direction with a lot of strength will continue on that path until the strength of the trend is lost.

The use of momentum trading can be traced back to the 1700s where the famous investor and British economist David Ricardo is said to have used momentum strategies successfully.

Relative momentum Vs. Absolute momentum: Momentum trading is largely used in two ways. The first is the relative momentum strategy, which is where the traders compare the performance of many securities in a particular class of assets. The traders will prefer to get strong performing securities and sell the weaker ones.

On the other hand, absolute momentum strategy is the performance of a security in the current moment is compared to the behavior in the past (historical time series). In foreign exchange trading, one can use either absolute or relative momentum. In most cases, momentum trading is associated with absolute momentum.

Employing the momentum trade style: Within-day trading momentum can be assessed over a time frame of minutes or even hours while in longer-term trading, it may be determined over longer periods, say weeks or months. When using the momentum strategy, the initial step that traders take involves identifying where the trend is headed (direction of the trade) and the one they wish to trade in. The traders may then use one of the indicators used in momentum analysis to seek and establish a point of entry to buy or sell the currency.

Further, a trader will want to assess a good point of exit, which is reasonable and profitable in the trade based on previously observed and projected levels of resistance and support in the market. Additionally, traders are advised to set a stop loss order either above or below the point of entry depending on the trade direction. This helps to safeguard against the chances of undesired losses and unexpected price trend reversals.

Momentum indicators: Many traders use the momentum indicator to determine the momentum of an asset. The indicator involves graphics devices that show how fast the prices of a given currency are moving in a certain direction. Usually, they are in the form of oscillators, and additionally, they indicate the probability of the price movement continuing on its trajectory.

There are some technical indicator tools that the traders use to track momentum and identify whether a particular entry or exit point is viable. They include Moving averages, relative strength index, moving average convergence divergence, stochastic, Commodity channel index, on balance volume, stochastic momentum index building block, and average directional index (ADX).

Reversal trading

A reversal occurs when the direction of an existing price trend rapidly changes directions abruptly to run parallel to the prevailing trend. On a price chart, reversals can be easily determined after they have hit the new point of resistance and dropped back the way they started. Reversals are also known as corrections, rallies, or trend reversals.

An uptrend, which is moving along with a series of higher lows and higher highs, will reverse into a downtrend and start showing a series of lower lows and lower highs. The opposite can be said of an existing downtrend. Reversals typically occur most frequently in intraday trading as long timeframes tend to smooth things out overall. These types of reversals can happen as part of a natural market correction, but are more commonly seen as the result of news releases or other occurrences that suddenly change the evaluation of a given stock.

By keeping a close eye on technical indicators, successful traders can often determine when a reversal is occurring before it has fully formed. Additionally, if a stock has been reaching record highs or lows, then it is often natural to assume that a reversal is at hand. Specifically, you will find candlestick movements useful when it comes to determining these shifts as quickly as possible. While many traders content themselves with successfully calling bottoms or tops, the best reversal traders only enter the field once the top or bottom has already formed. Trading reversals successfully often mean standing by as you wait for the perfect setup to unfold.

Mentally, it can be quite challenging to get into the reversal trading mindset because so many day traders are primed to make trades as quickly as possible when signals turn in their favor. Getting over this mental hump is key to successfully trading reversals in the long term.

In order to trade reversals successfully, it is important never to use pending orders when you know the price is approaching your target level. Additionally, you need to prepare yourself to miss out on a certain portion of the profits every time. This is an unavoidable part of the process and will ensure you win more than you lose in the long run.

Support and resistance trading

Swing trading: With swing trading, the goal is to identify the overall trend the stock is likely to take and then capture gains within that trend. Technical analysis is a natural fit here as a means by which traders can take advantage of the trend by ensuring their trades are as effective as possible. Swing trading is often riskier than investment trading and also includes higher commission costs as well. Successful swing traders tend to work the main trend that a chart is presenting at any given time. There are also swing trading opportunities that manifest when a specific stock begins to move back and forth between support and resistance points and swing traders will take long positions when the price reaches the support level and short positions when it nears the resistance level.

Due to the fact that stock market prices rarely move in a straight line, bullish swing traders typically need to look for initial upward movement as the primary part of a trend before expecting a reversal, otherwise known as a counter-trend. Once this counter-trend has successfully completed its arc, there should then be a resumption of upward movement. Since it is difficult to determine the length of the primary counter-trend, then you will want to enter into a bullish swing trade only once the counter-trend has ended and the uptrend has restarted.

With this out of the way, you should then be able to determine the ideal time to enter a specific trade by isolating the relevant movement of the counter-trend. An excellent way to do this is by determining when the stock trades at a price that is higher than the previous high. The entry point that you should find will then most likely be comparable to the price point from the previous few days as well in order to accurately determine risk as well as the potential upside for your target.

To do so, you are going to want to start by finding the lowest point of the counter-trend, which can be considered the stop-out point. If the stock drops past this point at some time in the future, you are going to want to exit the trade as quickly as possible in order to limit your possibility for losses. With this done, you will want to seek out the highest point on the uptrend before it became a counter-trend, as this point will be your profit target. If the stock returns to this price or rises above it, you are going to want to exit out a portion of your holdings in order to ensure that some level of gains are assured.

The difference between these points is going to be how much you can potentially expect to realistically make on the trade, while the difference between the entry and stop out points equaling the level of overall risk. When starting a swing trade, you are going to want to ensure that you are trading into a scenario where you have twice the chance to profit compared to the amount you are going to risk.

Once you have determined that it is worth the risk, you are going to want to enter a buy-stop limit order so that as soon as the stock hits the price of your entry point, the order will be activated and executed. Once the option is open, you would then want to enter a one-cancels-other order to sell the stock as soon as it hits either the stop-loss price or the price where you are happy taking your profits and running. Thus, as soon as one of the orders is executed, the other will be canceled.

Other types of trading

ABCD trading: The ABCD pattern is the chart pattern that is used for purposes of identifying potential long trades. This pattern is normally used for intraday trades, but can be applied to other different timeframes.

One of the characteristics of this chart pattern is the initial spike (A). During this spike, the stock price gets to the highest point of the day. Once this phase is over, there is a reasonable downward trend as investors seeking quick profits begin to get rid of their shares.

Later on, investors overwhelm sellers, and an intraday low position (B) gets established. It is at this juncture that the stock may indicate strength by setting a little higher than the intraday low position. This is now the higher low position (C).

The aim is basically to attain the initial (A) position to maximize profitability, but at the same time, to manage the risk, which means an exit at position (B). If the stock manages to break past point (A), the plan will have succeeded, and we take out profits at point (D).

The company's future earnings and potential are inconsequential at this stage. However, sometimes long trades may not place strong bullish charts. In other situations, the stock chart performs badly, though it may experience a small bounce before proceeding with the downward trend. You may get long during these small bounces, but not do so for too long.

CHAPTER 6:

Stock Scanning & Building a Watchlist

The U.S. stock exchanges contain more than eight thousand different listings. Despite the wide variety of options available when it comes to choosing viable stocks, most new day traders end up following the masses and sticking to just a few main stocks simply because they haven't taken the time they need to build a proper watchlist. This, in turn, is caused because stock scanning is a skill which means that, like any other skill, it can be developed over time with practice.

In order to generate the type of watchlist that will make an effort worthwhile, it is important to have an up-to-the-minute understanding of the current state of the market, the ways in which various capitalization levels directly influence the price development and also the multiple ways your chosen sectors react differently to the same influencing factors. What's more, market sentiment, seasonality, and economic cycles are all going to come into play as well when it comes to picking out the perfect choices to watch monthly, weekly, and daily. While it can be complicated to start, the rewards in both the long and short-term will most certainly be worth the effort.

Getting started

First things first, it is important to ensure that the requirements you determine for your watchlist are properly aligned with your personal trading plan. If you are only following a handful of positions per day, then you can afford to keep things simple with only around 75 listings to track per day while the day trader who is all-in might track as many as 500 stocks per day. Generally speaking, the average screen can hold about 75 issues, which means if you plan on day trading regularly, you are going to want to dedicate at least one screen just to the relevant tickers.

Create a personal database: The stocks that ultimately get the most face time on your trading screens tend to come from several sources, but the main feeder for such things should be your personal database while your daily routine should allow you to replenish those leads that ultimately come to fruition. Carefully maintaining your database should make it possible to also regularly cull your list of some stocks that may have seen a shift in the market, or have simply fallen out of favor. This is why your database must be tightly managed with rules that dictate not just when things should be added to your list, but when they should be subtracted as well.

To start your database, you can go with several common market leaders or other stocks that you have already had some success following in the short-term. You can find sector lists of various major players online and possibly already listed as part of your trading platform or charting software. During this time, it is important that you avoid any issues that are being thinly traded as most spreads of this type aren't going to be particularly well-suited to the type of active trading you are going to be pursuing.

The next step is then to create a list of the stocks that you are looking to prioritize - no matter what - as this can be a separate group in your list that remains on your radar. It is important to pick stocks from all sectors, even those you are not currently interested in as doing so will allow you to keep tabs on choices for the future should your current plans fall through.

Scanning for success: Once you have a database started, the next step is going to be scanning the market to ensure that the stocks you add to your list meet the correct criteria for success. Once you add in the types of criteria that naturally fits your trading style, you will have successfully generated the type of list that you can check daily for the types of patterns that will lead you to greater success in the long-term. Many trading platforms and charting services provide a related function, but you may want to seek out personalized software if you are going to move beyond the 75 stocks per day window into the realm of the true professional.

When creating your scanning criteria, it is essential to avoid being overly specific as the objective should be to identify stocks that might be trending in a useful direction, not those that are ready to go right now. Your nightly scan should give you a focus for the next day, not provide you with out and out winners. The details you find should likely provide you with levels of support and resistance that warrant a closer look in the future.

From there, you can then combine basic analysis and the strategies discussed in the previous chapters to find the types of stocks that are likely to be seeing more and more attention in the coming weeks. As an example, if your scan were to include the price when compared to the 26-day EMA as well as earnings from the last quarter, you could easily come across the same stocks that the professionals are sure to be eying sooner or later, and thus successfully beat them to the punch.

Common ways to scan the market include candlesticks that identify single-bar reversals. Patterns that tend to signal change either high or low and indicators that point out odd activity are all good choices as well.

www.ingramcontent.com/pod-product-compliance
Lightning Source LLC
Chambersburg PA
CBHW020616220526
45463CB00006B/2600